1

Copyright CJLuvBooks
Copyright text and design: Cherie Love
Copyright Editing: Jacquelyn Nicholson
All rights reserved. Without limiting the rights above.
No part of this publication may be reproduced or
transmitted in any form or by any means (electronic,
mechanical, photocopying, recording or otherwise)
without the prior written permission of both the copyright
owner and publisher of this book.

The photographs in this book have been included to
enhance the reader's overall experience. Any relationship
between the photographs and the subject matter is purely
coincidental.

Copyright 2022 by the author of this book.

The book author retains sole copyright to her contribution
to this book.

The Blurb provided layout designs and graphic elements
are copyright Blurb inc. 2022.

This book was created using the Blurb creative publishing
service. The book author retains sole right to her
contribution to this book.

Introduction

I have written this little book to bless you and to help you focus on the goodness of God through practicing gratefulness.

Even the world understands the benefits of being grateful and I think if anything, God's People are a little behind the eight ball in this respect.

We should be thankful to God of-course, for all the wonderful; things He has done for us, however if we just focus on God's Hands (what we get out of it) compared to His Face (who He is) then we are missing the best part of the Lord.

In order to truly worship, we must know WHO we are worshipping. His character and His ways. I think practicing gratefulness shifts our focus from worldly matters to heavenly ones. and it helps us to become intimately acquainted with the Lord. in a way that otherwise we wouldn't perceive.. It blesses us to be thankful and it pleases God also!

I hope you enjoy my little book, as much as I enjoyed creating it! Why not buy one for a friend as well? I keep my profits extremely low in order for you to be able to afford this book.

Love and Blessings,

Cherie

My Little Book of Gratitude

Being Grateful opens a door
for more of God's Grace.

PRAYER

Dear Father, thank You that I can come to you today and share my joys and my burdens with You. Thank You that You always hear my prayers of thankfulness. Being grateful must turn into a way of life for me, not just to pray occasionally!!
Help me with this Lord; I know You are always watching over me and I am very grateful for that!
I do believe that Your Favour rests on those who are obedient to Your Word, and that includes practicing gratefulness.

My Little Book of Gratitude

Practicing Gratefulness and refusing to be bitter, makes it easier for those around you.

PRAYER

Father, I know that sometimes I get frustrated and disappointed which can easily turn to bitterness and no-one wants to be around a bitter person, including You!
I take a moment now, to check my heart and see 'if there is any wayward way within me.'
I pull all roots of bitterness out of my soul which may be lurking there, and I thank You for Your Grace and Forgiveness today.

My Little Book of Gratitude

Being Grateful in the good days and the bad, helps us to remain hidden in Christ.

PRAYER

I thank You so much Jesus that the power of sin is broken over me because You have raised me up to be seated with You in heavenly places.
My previous way of life has been put to death and now I live a glorious life hidden in You. When You look at me Father, You no longer see my sin because I am now a new creation thanks to Your Son's death and resurrection. How grateful I am for this Lord!

My Little Book of Gratitude

Being Grateful strengthens
our walk with God.

PRAYER

How can I not be strengthened as I read Your Word and worship and pray to You every day!! Your Word is alive and active and shows me the thoughts and intents of my heart.
I thank You Lord that You are my strength and shield and my fortress. When I am grateful towards You, it strengthens our bond of intimacy.
What a great God and loving Father You are!

My Little Book of Gratitude

Being Grateful helps us to stay on track.

PRAYER

Some days are harder than others for staying on track with You Holy Spirit. Some days I miss Your direction because I am too busy to pray.
Thank You that Your mercies are new every morning and that You guide me and teach me through Your Word.
Help me to be faithful to You so that You can keep me on track all through my life.
"Lord, You alone are my portion and my cup, You make my lot secure." (Ps. 16:5)

My Little Book of Gratitude

Find something to be grateful for, even when you are going through a fiery trial.

PRAYER

Lord I confess that it is hard for me to find something positive in my day when everything around me is chaos.
When everything in my life is going wrong, I sometimes find it hard to be grateful.
Then I remember Habakkuk saying that even though the fig tree does not bud and the crops fail and there is no livestock in the pens, "Yet will I rejoice in the Lord, I will be joyful in God my Saviour."
(Hab. 3:17,18)
Thank You for that reminder today!

My Little Book of Gratitude

Practice Thankfulness,
because your turn around
could be just around the
corner.

PRAYER

Dear Father, help me to remember Your goodness and kindness towards me and that You will never leave me nor forsake me.
I need to know that when I am waiting for Your promises to manifest.
I will be steadfast and look to You daily with thankfulness in my heart because I know that You are a faithful God, and my turn-around is just around the corner.
I will practice being grateful even when I can't see the forest for the trees and I will trust Your timing.

My Little Book of Gratitude

Being Grateful may be that last little piece to give you a breakthrough.

PRAYER

I need a breakthrough Lord,
and sometimes I despair that
it will ever come!
I forget that none of Your
Words fall to the ground and
that Your promises spoken to
me will eventually come to
pass.
I am so grateful that You are
teaching me many precious
life lessons while I wait.
I will continue to thank You
every day for the sunshine,
the rain and the cloudy days,
because I know that Your
intentions are always good
towards me.

My Little Book of Gratitude

Being Grateful keeps us steady.

PRAYER

Dear Jesus, keep me steady in You. Keep my head above water because some days I feel like I am drowning. I would have despaired if I had not experienced Your goodness in this life. You are my rock. The only One I know.
All around me is sinking sand, but when my gaze alights on You Lord, then I feel and know that You are an anchor for my soul.

My Little Book of Gratitude

Being Grateful helps us to focus "on the things above." (Col. 3:1)

PRAYER

Your Word tells us to focus on the things above; on heavenly matters, not earthly ones.
How easy it is to turn my gaze away from that to the problems around me, which want to choke the life out of me.
Help me to see things from Your perspective Lord, and to not be distracted by the evil in the world. Let Your love abound to me as I meditate on Your Word which brings life to my mortal soul and shows me the way to live.

My Little Book of Gratitude

It is SO important to develop Thankfulness. Being Grateful Keeps bitterness away.

PRAYER

It is so important for me to practice gratefulness every day Lord, because I know it keeps a root of bitterness away. I have seen how horrible it is to deal with a bitter person and I never want to be like that. Help me in this area, because sometimes it seems like life is against me and I feel bitterness creeping in. Help me to be aware of my own attitudes at all times and to know that You are in charge of my life and You will keep me from harm.

My Little Book of Gratitude

Being Grateful helps us to lock into God's Promises.

PRAYER

Thank You Father, that every answer in Christ Jesus is 'Yes' and 'Amen'. Thank You for the promises You have spoken over my life. Help me to believe by faith, that every single one will come true. When I am grateful for all You have done in my life, it gives me impetus for the next thing that You are doing. You have good plans for my life to give me a hope and a future and I put ,y trust completely in You today.

My Little Book of Gratitude

Being Grateful help us to focus on the Goodness of God, and not on those things around us.

PRAYER

Dear Father, it is so easy for me to forget Your Goodness, when everything in my life is topsy-turvy. It makes me forget that You are the same yesterday, today and forever, and that Your mercies are new every morning.
You are good, and a stronghold in the day of trouble. Help me to remember that on days that are grey and dreary.
Your Goodness puts a smile on my face and joy in my heart!

My Little Book of Gratitude

Being Grateful helps us to know God's character.

PRAYER

Holy Spirit, as I set my heart
to practice gratefulness
every day, You in turn
illuminate my spirit and
soul to comprehend how
wide, how long, how high,
and how deep the love of
God is.
You live in me Holy Spirit,
to guide me into all truth
and to help me remember
all that God has said. You
reveal the character of God
to me and You always
point me to Jesus. How
thankful I am, that You are
living in my heart

Being Grateful releases more emotional energy than any other attitude. It releases endorphins into your system and lifts your mood.

PRAYER

Dear Father, how wonderful it is that You have made us so delicately but so resilient at the same time! "Being positive" isn't just words, but when I pray out Your life-giving scriptures it changes my attitude to life. . As an added bonus, You have made my body reflect this attitude by releasing feel-good hormones into my system. Thank You for showing me this, so that I can see the benefit of practicing gratefulness every day.

My Little Book of Gratitude

Being Grateful shows others our faith and trust in God.

PRAYER

Dear Lord Jesus, when I am feeling overwhelmed, You lead me to the Rock that is higher than I. I am so grateful that I can trust You in every circumstance of my life. Please help me to show my faith in You to those around me and to reflect Your glorious light, especially when things get tough. What a great witness it is to others when I can do that.

My Little Book of Gratitude

Being Grateful keeps us focused on God's Love and Mercy.

PRAYER

Dear Father I am so very grateful for Your love and mercy.
I mess up sometimes, but it is such a relief when I lift up my voice in a cry of repentance, knowing that You hear me and forgive me.
You have made every provision on the Cross of Calvary to redeem me.
What grace and mercy You show to Your child!!
Thank You!

My Little Book of Gratitude

Being Grateful helps us
to know God's Provision
and Power.

PRAYER

Thank You today Jesus
for Your provision in
every area of my life.
I know that You already
know what I need, but
You wish for us to ask so
that we partner with
You in all things.
Every good gift comes
from You Lord: this I
know and I am always
so grateful to You that I
can trust You to provide
for me and my family.

My Little Book of Gratitude

Practicing Thankfulness
makes us less self-centred.

PRAYER

Thank You Father, that
when I choose to look at
You and not myself, then
everything becomes a little
clearer.
Teach me to be grateful
when I am being
self-centred and selfish.
I truly don't want to act in
these ways and I thank
You today, that You have
revealed to me the areas in
which I need to change.
I place all my ego at the
foot of the Cross and choose
to be thankful today for
who I am in You.

My Little Book of Gratitude

Being Grateful reminds
us that the little things
in life DO matter.

PRAYER

Dear Jesus, when I look full into Your wonderful Face, nothing else in life matters. How important it is for me to meet with You every single day to experience Your Love and Your Presence. It keeps my focus on the little blessings in my life, which I can overlook because of busyness and frustration.
Let me take a breath now, to lift up my prayers of thankfulness to You for the myriad ways You bless me.

Cherie Love is an inspired teacher and preacher who has a heart to draw people together from all Christian cultures and encourage them into a deeper walk with our Lord Jesus. She loves to teach people how to draw closer to God and flow in a Prophetic anointing.

She has been a Leader in Children's Ministry, Prayer and Intercession Groups as well as Ladies Home Cells. Cherie is the founder of Ignite Warrior Women and Ignite W.W. Adelaide on Facebook and you can also find her at Cherie Love Author Page and Cherie Love Ministry Page. She currently preaches at her local Church, as well as being involved in Pastoral ministry as the Women's Ministry Leader. She was a Chaplain for 15 years at two primary schools and is a professional Counsellor. Walking along the beach and having hot chocolates at local cafes is her favourite thing to do to relax. Cherie has a husband and two sons, one daughter-in-law and two beautiful grandsons, and she loves to have family gatherings whenever possible!!! Chocolate is her Achille's heel, but we won't mention that too loudly!!! Shhhhhh!!!

Other Books by Cherie

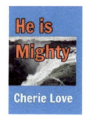

47

CPSIA information can be obtained
at www.ICGtesting.com
Printed in the USA
BVHW020845071122
651333BV00016B/299/J